The
Best Love
Poems
Ever

The Adventures of Tom Sawyer
by Mark Twain
with an introduction by
Jean Craighead George

Anne of Avonlea
by L.M. Montgomery
with an introduction by
Jennifer L. Holm

Anne of Green Gables
by L.M. Montgomery
with an introduction by
Anne Mazer

The Best Poems Ever
edited by Edric S. Mesmer

Black Beauty
by Anna Sewell
with an introduction by
Gail Carson Levine

The Call of the Wild
by Jack London
with an introduction by
Avi

A Christmas Carol
by Charles Dickens
with an introduction by
Karen Hesse

Dr. Jekyll and Mr. Hyde and
Other Stories of the
Supernatural
by Robert Louis Stevenson
with an introduction by
Garth Nix

Dracula
by Bram Stoker
with an introduction by
Walter Dean Myers

The Gift of the Magi
and Other Stories
by O. Henry
with an introduction by
Pam Muñoz Ryan

Great Expectations
by Charles Dickens
with an introduction by
Michael Cadnum

Kidnapped
by Robert Louis Stevenson
with an introduction by
Sid Hite

A Little Princess
by Frances Hodgson Burnett
with an introduction by
E.L. Konigsburg

Little Women
by Louisa May Alcott
with an introduction by
Paula Danziger

Peter Pan
by J.M. Barrie
with an introduction by
Jack Gantos

Pride and Prejudice
by Jane Austen
with an introduction by
Katherine Paterson

The Best Love Poems Ever

a collection of poetry's most romantic voices

Edited by David Rohlfing

SCHOLASTIC INC.

New York Toronto London Auckland Sydney
Mexico City New Delhi Hong Kong Buenos Aires

ISBN 0-439-45345-3

Permissions are located on pages 65 and 66.

12 11 10 9 8 7 6 5 4 3 2 1   3 4 5 6 7 8/0

Printed in the U.S.A.   01

First Scholastic printing, January 2003

TABLE OF CONTENTS

HAPPENSTANCE

Rita Dove

When you appeared it was as if
magnets cleared the air.
I had never seen that smile before
or your hair, flying silver. Someone
waving goodbye, she was silver, too.
Of course you didn't see me.
I called softly so you could choose
not to answer — then called again.
You turned in the light, your eyes
seeking your name.

AMONG THE MULTITUDE

Walt Whitman

Among the men and women the multitude,
I perceive one picking me out by secret and
      divine signs,
Acknowledging none else, not parent, wife, husband,
      brother, child, any nearer than I am,
Some are baffled, but that one is not — that one
      knows me.

Ah lover and perfect equal,
I meant that you should discover me so by faint
      indirections,
And I when I meet you mean to discover you
      by the like in you.

THERE IS A LADY SWEET AND KIND

Anonymous

There is a lady sweet and kind,
Was never face so pleased my mind;
I did but see her passing by,
And yet I love her till I die.

Her gesture, motion and her smiles,
Her wit, her voice, my heart beguiles,
Beguiles my heart, I know not why,
And yet I love her till I die.

Her free behavior, winning looks,
Will make a lawyer burn his books.
I touched her not, alas, not I,
And yet I love her till I die.

Had I her fast betwixt mine arms,
Judge you that think such sports were harms,
Were't any harm? No, no, fie, fie!
For I will love her till I die.

Should I remain confinèd there,
So long as Phoebus in his sphere,

I to request, she to deny,
Yet would I love her till I die.

Cupid is wingèd and doth range;
Her country so my love doth change,
But change she earth, or change she sky,
Yet will I love her till I die.

TO MISTRESS MARGARET HUSSEY

John Skelton

Merry Margaret,
   As midsummer flower,
Gentle as falcon
Or hawk of the tower:
With solace and gladness,
Much mirth and no madness,
All good and no badness;
     So joyously,
     So maidenly,
     So womanly
     Her demeaning
     In every thing,
     Far, far passing
     That I can indite,
     Or suffice to write
Of Merry Margaret
   As midsummer flower,
Gentle as falcon
Or hawk of the tower.
   As patient and still
And as full of good will
As fair Isaphill,

Coriander,
Sweet pomander,
Good Cassander,
Steadfast of thought,
Well made, well wrought,
Far may be sought
Ere that ye can find
So courteous, so kind
As Merry Margaret,
   This midsummer flower,
Gentle as falcon
Or hawk of the tower.

from The Garlande of Laurell

SPRING, THE SWEET SPRING

Thomas Nashe

Spring, the sweet spring, is the year's pleasant king;
Then blooms each thing, then maids dance in a ring,
Cold doth not sting, the pretty birds do sing,
    "Cuckoo, jug-jug, pu-we, to-witta-woo!"

The palm and may make country houses gay,
Lambs frisk and play, the shepherds pipe all day,
And we hear aye birds tune this merry lay,
    "Cuckoo, jug-jug, pu-we, to-witta-woo!"

The fields breathe sweet, the daisies kiss our feet,
Young lovers meet, old wives a-sunning sit,
In every street these tunes our ears do greet,
    "Cuckoo, jug-jug, pu-we, to-witta-woo!"
    Spring, the sweet spring!

from Summer's Last Will and Testament

THE PASSIONATE SHEPHERD TO HIS LOVE

Christopher Marlowe

Come live with me and be my love,
And we will all the pleasures prove,
That valleys, groves, hills, and fields,
Woods, or steepy mountain yields.

And we will sit upon the rocks,
Seeing the shepherds feed their flocks,
By shallow rivers, to whose falls
Melodious birds sing madrigals.

And I will make thee beds of roses,
And a thousand fragrant posies,
A cap of flowers and a kirtle
Embroider'd all with leaves of myrtle.

A gown made of the finest wool,
Which from our pretty lambs we pull;
Fair linèd slippers for the cold,
With buckles of the purest gold.

A belt of straw and ivy buds,
With coral clasps and amber studs:

And if these pleasures may thee move,
Come live with me and be my love.

The shepherd swains shall dance and sing
For thy delight each May morning:
If these delights thy mind may move,
Then live with me and be my love.

THE NYMPH'S REPLY TO THE SHEPHERD

Sir Walter Raleigh

If all the world and love were young,
And truth in every shepherd's tongue,
These pretty pleasures might me move
To live with thee and be thy love.

Time drives the flocks from field to fold,
When rivers rage and rocks grow cold,
And Philomel becometh dumb;
The rest complains of cares to come.

The flowers do fade, and wanton fields
To wayward winter reckoning yields;
A honey tongue, a heart of gall,
Is fancy's spring, but sorrow's fall.

Thy gowns, thy shoes, thy beds of roses,
Thy cap, thy kirtle, and thy posies
Soon break, soon wither, soon forgotten, —
In folly ripe, in reason rotten.

Thy belt of straw and ivy buds,
The coral clasps and amber studs,

All these in me no means can move
To come to thee and be thy love.

But could youth last and love still breed,
Had joys no date nor age no need,
Then these delights my mind might move
To live with thee and be thy love.

QUESTIONS FOR THE MOON

Ho Xuan Huong

How many thousands of years have you been there?
Why sometimes slender, sometimes full?

How old is the White Rabbit?
How many children belong to Moon-Girl?

Why do you circle the purple loneliness of night
and seldom blush before the sun?

Weary, past midnight, who are you searching for?
Are you in love with these rivers and hills?

translated from the Nom and Vietnamese by John Balaban

THE LOOK

Sara Teasdale

Strephon kissed me in the spring,
   Robin in the fall,
But Colin only looked at me
   And never kissed at all.

Strephon's kiss was lost in jest,
   Robin's lost in play,
But the kiss in Colin's eyes
   Haunts me night and day.

FIRST LOVE

John Clare

I ne'er was struck before that hour
  With love so sudden and so sweet,
Her face it bloomed like a sweet flower
  And stole my heart away complete.
My face turned pale as deadly pale,
  My legs refused to walk away,
And when she looked, what could I ail?
  My life and all seemed turned to clay.

And then my blood rushed to my face
  And took my eyesight quite away,
The trees and bushes round the place
  Seemed midnight at noonday.
I could not see a single thing,
  Words from my eyes did start —
They spoke as chords do from the string,
  And blood burnt round my heart.

Are flowers the winter's choice?
  Is love's bed always snow?
She seemed to hear my silent voice,
  Not love's appeals to know.
I never saw so sweet a face

As that I stood before.
My heart has left its dwelling-place
And can return no more.

(UNTITLED)

Meera

My friend,
     I'm head
over heels.

His form,
     his lotus eyes
his glance which isn't
all that straight

have carved themselves
upon my sight.

     On the banks
of the Jumna
     he grazed
his cows and played

low notes, and I

I dropped the veils
of thought

       and ran

and fled

      and took shelter
at His feet.

translated from the Hindi by Shama Futehally

SHE WALKS IN BEAUTY

Lord Byron

She walks in beauty, like the night
    Of cloudless climes and starry skies;
And all that's best of dark and bright
    Meet in her aspect and her eyes:
Thus mellowed to that tender light
    Which heaven to gaudy day denies.

One shade the more, one ray the less,
    Had half impaired the nameless grace
Which waves in every raven tress,
    Or softly lightens o'er her face;
Where thoughts serenely sweet express
    How pure, how dear their dwelling place.

And on that cheek, and o'er that brow,
    So soft, so calm, yet eloquent,
The smiles that win, the tints that glow,
    But tell of days in goodness spent,
A mind at peace with all below,
    A heart whose love is innocent!

SYMPTOMS OF LOVE

Robert Graves

Love is a universal migraine,
A bright stain on the vision
Blotting out reason.

Symptoms of true love
Are leanness, jealousy,
Laggard dawns;

Are omens and nightmares —
Listening for a knock,
Waiting for a sign:

For a touch of her fingers
In a darkened room,
For a searching look.

Take courage, lover!
Could you endure such grief
At any hand but hers?

(UNTITLED)

Sappho

It's no use

Mother dear, I
can't finish my
weaving
        You may
blame Aphrodite

soft as she is

she has almost
killed me with
love for that boy

translated from the Greek by Mary Barnard

MEETING AT NIGHT

Robert Browning

The gray sea and the long black land;
And the yellow half-moon large and low;
And the startled little waves that leap
In fiery ringlets from their sleep,
As I gain the cove with pushing prow,
And quench its speed i' the slushy sand.
Then a mile of warm sea-scented beach;
Three fields to cross till a farm appears;
A tap at the pane, the quick sharp scratch
And blue spurt of a light match,
And a voice less loud, through its joys and fears,
Than the two hearts beating each to each!

A BIRTHDAY

Christina Rossetti

My heart is like a singing bird
   Whose nest is in a watered shoot;
My heart is like an apple-tree
   Whose boughs are bent with thickset fruit;
My heart is like a rainbow shell
   That paddles in a halcyon sea;
My heart is gladder than all these
   Because my love is come to me.

Raise me a dais of silk and down;
   Hang it with vair and purple dyes;
Carve it in doves and pomegranates,
   And peacocks with a hundred eyes;
Work it in gold and silver grapes,
   In leaves and silver fleurs-de-lys;
Because the birthday of my life
   Is come, my love is come to me.

A NEGRO LOVE SONG

Paul Laurence Dunbar

Seen my lady home las' night,
   Jump back, honey, jump back.
Hel' huh han' an' sque'z it tight,
   Jump back, honey, jump back.
Hyeahd huh sigh a little sigh,
Seen a light gleam f'om huh eye,
An' a smile go flittin' by —
   Jump back, honey, jump back.

Hyeahd de win' blow thoo de pine,
   Jump back, honey, jump back.
Mockin'-bird was singin'fine,
   Jump back, honey, jump back.
An' my hea't was beatin' so,
When I reached my lady's do',
Dat I couldn't ba' to go —
   Jump back, honey, jump back.

Put my ahm aroun' huh wais',
   Jump back, honey, jump back.
Raised huh lips an' took a tase,
   Jump back, honey, jump back.

Love me, honey, love me true?
Love me well ez I love you?
An' she answe'd "'Cose I do"—
  Jump back, honey, jump back.

THE YOUNGEST CHILDREN OF AN ANGEL

Anna Swir

When you kissed me for the first time
we became a couple
of the youngest children of an angel,
which just started
to fledge.

Lapsed into a silence in mid-move,
hushed in mid-breath,
astounded
to the very blood,
they listen with their bodies
to the sprouting on their shoulder blades
of the first little plume.

Translated from the Polish by Czeslaw Milosz and
Leonard Nathan

FROM BLOSSOMS

Li-Young Lee

From blossoms comes
this brown paper bag of peaches
we bought from the boy
at the bend in the road where we turned toward
signs painted *Peaches*.

From laden boughs, from hands,
from sweet fellowship in the bins,
comes nectar at the roadside, succulent
peaches we devour, dusty skin and all,
comes the familiar dust of summer, dust we eat.

O, to take what we love inside,
to carry within us an orchard, to eat
not only the skin, but the shade,
not only the sugar, but the days, to hold
the fruit in our hands, adore it, then bite into
the round jubilance of peach.

There are days we live
as if death were nowhere
in the background; from joy

to joy to joy, from wing to wing,
from blossom to blossom to
impossible blossom, to sweet impossible blossom.

TO ANTHEA WHO MAY COMMAND
HIM ANYTHING

Robert Herrick

Bid me to live, and I will live
 Thy Protestant to be:
Or bid me love, and I will give
 A loving heart to thee.

A heart as soft, a heart as kind,
 A heart as sound and free
As in the whole world thou canst find,
 That heart I'll give to thee.

Bid that heart stay, and it will stay,
 To honour thy decree:
Or bid it languish quite away,
 And 't shall do so for thee.

Bid me weep, and I will weep
 While I have eyes to see:
And, having none, yet I will keep
 A heart to weep for thee.

Bid me despair, and I'll despair
 Under that cypress tree:

Or bid me die, and I will dare
    E'en death to die for thee.

Thou art my life, my love, my heart,
    The very eyes of me,
Thou hast command of every part,
    To live and die for thee.

HER FACE   HER TONGUE   HER WYTT

Arthur Gorges

Her face
So faier
first bent
myne eye

Her tongue
So sweete
then drewe
myne eare

Her wytt
So sharpe
then hitt
my harte

Myne eye
to lyke
her face
doth leade

Myne eare
to learne
her tongue
doth teache

My harte
to love
her wytt
doth move

Her face
with beames
doth blynd
myne eye

Her tongue
with sounde
doth charm
myne eare

Her wytt
with arte
doth knitt
my harte

Myne eye
with lyfe
her face
doth feede

Myne eare
with hope
her tongue
doth feaste

My harte
with skill
her wytt
doth fyll

O face
with frownes
wronge not
myne eye

O tongue
with cheeks
vex nott
myne eare

O wytt
with smarte
wounde not
my harte

This eye
shall Joye
her face
to serve

This eare
shall yeald
her tongue
to truste

This harte
shall swear
her wytt
to feare.

LOVE ME NOT FOR COMELY GRACE

John Wilbye

Love me not for comely grace,
For my pleasing eye or face;
Nor for any outward part,
No, nor for my constant heart:
   For those may fail or turn to ill,
   So thou and I shall sever.
Keep therefore a true woman's eye,
And love me still, but know not why;
   So hast thou the same reason still
   To doat upon me ever.

From THE SONG OF SOLOMON

Chapter 2

I am the rose of Sharon, and the lily of the valleys.

As the lily among thorns, so is my love among the
    daughters.

As the apple tree among the trees of the wood, so is
    my beloved among the sons. I sat down under his
    shadow with great delight, and his fruit was sweet
    to my taste.

He brought me to the banqueting house, and his
    banner over me was love.

Stay me with flagons, comfort me with apples: for I
    am sick of love.

His left hand is under my head, and his right hand
    doth embrace me.

I charge you, O ye daughters of Jerusalem, by the
    roes, and by the hinds of the field, that ye stir not
    up, nor awake my love, till he please.

The voice of my beloved! behold, he cometh leaping
    upon the mountains, skipping upon the hills.

My beloved is like a roe or a young hart: behold, he
    standeth behind our wall, he looketh forth at the
    windows, showing himself through the lattice.

My beloved spake, and said unto me, Rise up, my
    love, my fair one, and come away.

For, lo, the winter is past, the rain is over and gone;
The flowers appear on the earth; the time of the
    singing of birds is come, and the voice of the turtle
    is heard in our land:
The fig tree putteth forth her green figs, and the
    vines with the tender grape give a good smell.
    Arise, my love, my fair one, and come away.
O my dove, that art in the clefts of the rock, in the
    secret places of the stairs, let me see thy
    countenance, let me hear thy voice; for sweet is thy
    voice, and thy countenance is comely.
Take us the foxes, the little foxes, that spoil the vines;
    for our vines have tender grapes.
My beloved is mine, and I am his: he feedeth among
    the lilies.
Until the day break, and the shadows flee away, turn,
    my beloved, and be thou like a roe or a young hart
    upon the mountains of Bether.

from the authorized version (1611)

ON A BANK AS I SAT FISHING

Sir Henry Wotton

And now all Nature seemed in love;
The lusty sap began to move;
New juice did stir the embracing vines;
And birds had drawn their Valentines:
The jealous trout, that low did lie,
Rose at a well-dissembled fly:
There stood my friend, with patient skill
Attending of his trembling quill.
Already were the eaves possessed
With the swift Pilgrim's daubèd nest.
The groves already did rejoice
In Philomel's triumphing voice.

   The showers were short, the weather mild,
The morning fresh, the evening smiled.

   Joan takes her neat-rubbed pail, and now
She trips to milk the sand-red cow;
Where for some sturdy foot-ball swain,
Joan strokes a sillabub or twain.

   The fields and gardens were beset
With Tulips, Crocus, Violet:
And now, though late, the modest Rose
Did more than half a blush disclose.

Thus all looked gay, all full of cheer,
To welcome the new-livery'd year.

THE SUN

Mary Oliver

Have you ever seen
anything
in your life
more wonderful

than the way the sun,
every evening,
relaxed and easy,
floats toward the horizon

and into the clouds or the hills,
or the rumpled sea,
and is gone —
and how it slides again

out of the blackness,
every morning,
on the other side of the world,
like a red flower

streaming upward on its heavenly oils,
say, on a morning in early summer,

at its perfect imperial distance —
and have you ever felt for anything

such wild love —
do you think there is anywhere, in any language,
a word billowing enough
for the pleasure

that fills you,
as the sun
reaches out,
as it warms you

as you stand there,
empty-handed —
or have you too
turned from this world —

or have you too
gone crazy
for power,
for things?

SONNET XVIII

William Shakespeare

Shall I compare thee to a summer's day?
Thou art more lovely and more temperate:
Rough winds do shake the darling buds of May,
And summer's lease hath all too short a date;
Sometime too hot the eye of heaven shines,
And often is his gold complexion dimm'd;
And every fair from fair sometime declines,
By chance or nature's changing course untrimm'd:
But thy eternal summer shall not fade
Nor lose possession of that fair thou ow'st;
Nor shall Death brag thou wand'rest in his shade,
When in eternal lines to time thou grow'st;
So long as men can breathe or eyes can see,
So long lives this, and this gives life to thee.

A RED, RED ROSE

Robert Burns

O my Luve's like a red, red rose,
   That's newly sprung in June;
O my Luve's like the melodie
   That's sweetly play'd in tune. —

As fair art thou, my bonie lass,
   So deep in luve am I;
And I will love thee still, my Dear,
   Till a' the seas gang dry. —

Till a' the seas gang dry, my Dear,
   And the rocks melt wi' the sun:
I will love thee still, my Dear,
   While the sands o' life shall run. —

And fare thee weel, my only Luve!
   And fare thee weel, a while!
And I will come again, my Luve,
   Tho' it were ten thousand mile!

LOVE SONG

Pablo Neruda

I love you, I love you, is my song
and here my silliness begins.

I love you, I love you my lung,
I love you, I love you my wild grapevine,
and if love is like wine:
you are my predilection
from your hands to your feet:
you are the wineglass of hereafter
and my bottle of destiny.

I love you forwards and backwards,
and I don't have the tone or timbre
to sing you my song,
my endless song.

On my violin that sings out of tune
my violin declares,
I love you, I love you my double bass,
my sweet woman, dark and clear,
my heart, my teeth,
my light and my spoon,

41

my salt of the dim week,
my clear windowpane moon.

translated from the Spanish by William O'Daly

SONNET XLIII, FROM THE PORTUGUESE

Elizabeth Barrett Browning

How do I love thee? Let me count the ways.
I love thee to the depth and breadth and height
My soul can reach, when feeling out of sight
For the ends of Being and ideal Grace.
I love thee to the level of every day's
Most quiet need, by sun and candlelight.
I love thee freely, as men strive for Right;
I love thee purely, as they turn from Praise.
I love thee with the passion put to use
In my old griefs, and with my childhood's faith.
I love thee with a love I seemed to lose
With my lost saints, — I love thee with the breath,
Smiles, tears, of all my life! — and, if God choose,
I shall but love thee better after death.

TO —

Percy Bysshe Shelley

One word is too often profaned
    For me to profane it,
One feeling too falsely disdained
    For thee to disdain it;
One hope is too like despair
    For prudence to smother,
And pity from thee more dear
    Than that from another.

I can give not what men call love,
    But wilt thou accept not
The worship the heart lifts above
    And the Heavens reject not, —
The desire of the moth for the star,
    Of the night for the morrow,
The devotion to something afar
    From the sphere of our sorrow?

LOVE SONG

William Carlos Williams

What have I to say to you
When we shall meet?
Yet —
I lie here thinking of you.

The stain of love
Is upon the world.
Yellow, yellow, yellow,
It eats into the leaves,
Smears with saffron
The horned branches that lean
Heavily
Against a smooth purple sky.

There is no light —
Only a honey-thick stain
That drips from leaf to leaf
And limb to limb,
Spoiling the colors
Of the whole world.

I am alone.
The weight of love

Has buoyed me up
Till my head
Knocks against the sky.

See me!
My hair is dripping with nectar —
Starlings carry it
On their black wings.
See, at last
My arms and my hands
Are lying idle.

How can I tell
If I shall ever love you again
As I do now?

TO MY DEAR AND LOVING HUSBAND

Anne Bradstreet

If ever two were one, then surely we.
If ever man were lov'd by wife, then thee;
If ever wife was happy in a man,
Compare with me ye women if you can.
I prize thy love more than whole Mines of gold,
Or all the riches that the East doth hold.
My love is such that Rivers cannot quench,
Nor ought but love from thee, give recompence.
Thy love is such I can no way repay,
The heavens reward thee manifold I pray.
Then while we live, in love let's so persever,
That when we live no more, we may live ever.

A STATUE OF EROS

Zenodotos

Who carved Love
      and placed him by
this fountain,
      thinking
he could control
      such fire
with water?

translated from the Greek by Peter Jay

(UNTITLED)

Sir John Suckling

Out upon it, I have loved
   Three whole days together;
And am like to love three more,
   If it hold fair weather.

Time shall moult away his wings
   Ere he shall discover
In the whole wide world again
   Such a constant lover.

But a pox upon't, no praise
   There is due at all to me:
Love with me had made no stays,
   Had it any been but she.

Had it any been but she
   And that very very face,
There had been at least ere this
   A dozen dozen in her place.

LOVE AND LIFE

Lord Rochester

All my past life is mine no more;
  The flying hours are gone,
Like transitory dreams given o'er
Whose images are kept in store
  By memory alone.

Whatever is to come is not:
  How can it then be mine?
The present moment's all my lot,
And that, as fast as it is got,
  Phyllis, is wholly thine.

Then talk not of inconstancy,
  False hearts, and broken vows;
If I, by miracle, can be
This livelong minute true to thee,
  'Tis all that heaven allows.

NEVER SEEK TO TELL THY LOVE

William Blake

Never seek to tell thy love,
Love that never told can be;
For the gentle wind does move
Silently, invisibly.

I told my love, I told my love,
I told her all my heart;
Trembling, cold, in ghastly fears,
Oh! she doth depart.

Soon as she was gone from me,
A traveller came by,
Silently, invisibly:
He took her with a sigh.

(UNTITLED)

Bhartrhari

She who is always in my thoughts prefers
Another man, and does not think of me.
Yet he seeks for another's love, not hers;
And some poor girl is grieving for my sake.
   Why then, the devil take
Both her and him; and love; and her; and me.

Translated from the Sanskrit by John Brough

SINCE THERE'S NO HELP, COME LET US KISS AND PART

Michael Drayton

Since there's no help, come let us kiss and part;
Nay, I have done, you get no more of me,
And I am glad, yea, glad with all my heart
That thus so cleanly I myself can free;
Shake hands for ever, cancel all our vows,
And when we meet at any time again,
Be it not seen in either of our brows
That we one jot of former love retain.
Now at the last gasp of Love's latest breath,
When, his pulse failing, Passion speechless lies,
When Faith is kneeling by his bed of death,
And Innocence is closing up his eyes,
    Now if thou wouldst, when all have given him over,
    From death to life thou mightst him yet recover.

A VALEDICTION

Ernest Dowson

If we must part,
   Then let it be like this;
Not heart on heart,
   Nor with the useless anguish of a kiss;
But touch mine hand and say;
'Until tomorrow or some other day,
   If we must part.'

Words are so weak
   When love hath been so strong:
Let silence speak:
   'Life is a little while, and love is long;
A time to sow and reap,
And after harvest a long time to sleep,
   But words are weak.'

(UNTITLED)

A. E. Housman

Oh, when I was in love with you,
   Then I was clean and brave,
And miles around the wonder grew
   How well did I behave.

And now the fancy passes by,
   And nothing will remain,
And miles around they'll say that I
   Am quite myself again.

LOVE THOU ART HIGH

Emily Dickinson

Love — thou art high —
I cannot climb thee —
But, were it Two —
Who knows but we —
Taking turns — at the Chimborazo —
Ducal — at last — stand up by thee —

Love — thou art deep —
I cannot cross thee —
But, were there Two
Instead of One —
Rower, and Yacht — some sovereign Summer —
Who knows — but we'd reach the Sun?

Love — thou art Veiled —
A few — behold thee —
Smile — and alter — and prattle — and die —
Bliss — were an Oddity — without thee —
Nicknamed by God —
Eternity —

THEN

Muriel Rukeyser

When I am dead, even then,
I will still love you, I will wait in these poems,
When I am dead, even then
I am still listening to you.
I will still be making poems for you
out of silence;
silence will be falling into that silence,
it is building music.

(UNTITLED)

Edna St. Vincent Millay

What lips my lips have kissed, and where, and why,
I have forgotten, and what arms have lain
Under my head till morning; but the rain
Is full of ghosts tonight, that tap and sigh
Upon the glass and listen for reply,
And in my heart there stirs a quiet pain
For unremembered lads that not again
Will turn to me at midnight with a cry.
Thus in the winter stands the lonely tree,
Nor knows what birds have vanished one by one,
Yet knows its boughs more silent than before:
I cannot say what loves have come and gone;
I only know that summer sang in me
A little while, that in me sings no more.

TO ONE IN PARADISE

Edgar Allan Poe

Thou wast that all to me, love,
   For which my soul did pine —
A green isle in the sea, love,
   A fountain and a shrine,
All wreathed with fairy fruits and flowers,
   And all the flowers were mine.

Ah, dream too bright to last!
   Ah, starry Hope! that didst arise
But to be overcast!
   A voice from out the Future cries,
'On! on!' — but o'er the Past
   (Dim gulf!) my spirit hovering lies
Mute, motionless, aghast!

For, alas! alas! with me
   The light of Life is o'er!
   No more — no more — no more —
(Such language holds the solemn sea
   To the sands upon the shore)
Shall bloom the thunder-blasted tree,
   Or the stricken eagle soar!

And all my days are trances,
   And all my nightly dreams
And where thy grey eye glances,
   And where thy footstep gleams —
In what ethereal dances,
   By what eternal streams.

WHEN YOU ARE OLD

William Butler Yeats

When you are old and gray and full of sleep,
And nodding by the fire, take down this book,
And slowly read, and dream of the soft look
Your eyes had once, and of their shadows deep;

How many loved your moments of glad grace,
And loved your beauty with love false or true;
But one man loved the pilgrim soul in you,
And loved the sorrows of your changing face.

And bending down beside the glowing bars
Murmur, a little sadly, how love fled
And paced upon the mountains overhead
And hid his face amid a crowd of stars.

JENNY KISS'D ME

Leigh Hunt

Jenny kiss'd me when we met,
　　Jumping from the chair she sat in;
Time, you thief, who love to get
　　Sweets into your list, put that in!
Say I'm weary, say I'm sad,
　　Say that health and wealth have miss'd me,
Say I'm growing old, but add,
　　Jenny kiss'd me.

THE RING

Langston Hughes

Love is the master of the ring
And life a circus tent.
What is this silly song you sing?
Love is the master of the ring.

I am afraid!
Afraid of Love
And of Love's bitter whip!
Afraid,
Afraid of Love
And Love's sharp, stinging whip.

What is this silly song you sing?
Love is the master of the ring.

PERMISSIONS

INDEX OF AUTHORS AND TRANSLATORS